Romantic Attraction

CAUSES & EFFECTS
OF EMOTIONS

CAUSES & EFFECTS OF EMOTIONS

Romantic Attraction

Z.B. Hill

Mason Crest

Mason Crest
450 Parkway Drive, Suite D
Broomall, PA 19008
www.masoncrest.com

Printed and bound in the United States of America.

First printing
9 8 7 6 5 4 3 2 1

Series ISBN: 978-1-4222-3067-1
ISBN: 978-1-4222-3077-0
ebook ISBN: 978-1-4222-8770-5

Library of Congress Cataloging-in-Publication Data

Hill, Z. B.
  Romantic attraction / Z.B. Hill.
    pages cm. — (Causes & effects of emotions)
  Includes index.
  ISBN 978-1-4222-3077-0 (hardback)
  1. Sexual attraction—Juvenile literature. 2. Interpersonal attraction—Juvenile literature. 3. Man-woman relationships—Juvenile literature. 4. Sex—Juvenile literature I. Title.
  HQ784.S45H55 2015
  306.7—dc23
                                        2014004383

CONTENTS

KEY ICONS TO LOOK FOR:

Text-Dependent Questions: These questions send the reader back to the text for more careful attention to the evidence presented there.

Words to Understand: These words with their easy-to-understand definitions will increase the reader's understanding of the text, while building vocabulary skills.

Series Glossary of Key Terms: This back-of-the book glossary contains terminology used throughout this series. Words found here increase the reader's ability to read and comprehend higher-level books and articles in this field.

Research Projects: Readers are pointed toward areas of further inquiry connected to each chapter. Suggestions are provided for projects that encourage deeper research and analysis.

Sidebars: This boxed material within the main text allows readers to build knowledge, gain insights, explore possibilities, and broaden their perspectives by weaving together additional information to provide realistic and holistic perspectives.

INTRODUCTION

The journey of self-discovery for young adults can be a passage that includes times of introspection as well joyful experiences. It can also be a complicated route filled with confusing road signs and hazards along the way. The choices teens make will have lifelong impacts. From early romantic relationships to complex feelings of anxiousness, loneliness, and compassion, this series of books is designed specifically for young adults, tackling many of the challenges facing them as they navigate the social and emotional world around and within them. Each chapter explores the social emotional pitfalls and triumphs of young adults, using stories in which readers will see themselves reflected.

Adolescents encounter compound issues today in home, school, and community. Many young adults may feel ill equipped to identify and manage the broad range of emotions they experience as their minds and bodies change and grow. They face many adult problems without the knowledge and tools needed to find satisfactory solutions. Where do they fit in? Why are they afraid? Do others feel as lonely and lost as they do? How do they handle the emotions that can engulf them when a friend betrays them or they fail to make the grade? These are all important questions that young adults may face. Young adults need guidance to pilot their way through changing feelings that are influenced by peers, family relationships, and an ever-changing world. They need to know that they share common strengths and pressures with their peers. Realizing they are not alone with their questions can help them develop important attributes of resilience and hope.

The books in this series skillfully capture young people's everyday, real-life emotional journeys and provides practical and meaningful information that can offer hope to all who read them.

It covers topics that teens may be hesitant to discuss with others, giving them a context for their own feelings and relationships. It is an essential tool to help young adults understand themselves and their place in the world around them—and a valuable asset for teachers and counselors working to help young people become healthy, confident, and compassionate members of our society.

Cindy Croft, M.A.Ed
Director of the Center for Inclusive Child Care at Concordia University

Words to Understand

adolescence: The period of time during and after puberty, when a child develops into an adult.

biological: Having to do with living things and the way they work.

ONE

WHAT IS ROMANTIC ATTRACTION?

It's the first day of school, and thirteen-year-old Sarah is getting ready for the day. She's standing in front of her bathroom mirror, putting her hair up, frowning at it, and then putting it back down. She's bought new clothes for the new school year and she can't decide which top she likes best—the red one or the blue one. Usually, it only takes her a few minutes to get ready to leave the house. But today is different; today she knows she'll be seeing lots of friends she hasn't seen all summer. And she knows that she'll be seeing Matt today.

Her mom yells from down the hall that breakfast is getting cold. Sarah sighs and grabs her blue top. She leaves her hair down and smiles at herself in the mirror: she decides she looks beautiful. She's ready for the day!

At school, everyone is talking quickly in loud and excited

ROMANTIC ATTRACTION

Figuring out your relationships with the opposite sex can be tricky at any age.

voices. Sarah and her friends clump together around Jessica's locker, laughing and exchanging news from the summer months. But the biggest topic of the day is the upcoming school dance.

Ugh, thinks Sarah, *school has barely even begun and already we have to worry about a school dance.* Sarah has never liked school dances. They almost always end with someone crying or going home with hurt feelings. And yet you have to go or you look weird.

Jessica turns her attention on Sarah, and asks, "So, Sarah, do you think that Matt will ask you to the dance?"

Sarah cringes. How does Jessica know about her feelings for Matt? Even Sarah isn't sure how she feels about him. "Uh . . . I don't know. I guess he can do what he wants." This makes everyone laugh, and Sarah walks away feeling confused and a little hurt. Do they know something that she doesn't? Are they suggesting that she has a *crush* on Matt?

And yet Sarah can't help but admit, if only to herself, that she spends a lot of time lately thinking about Matt. Until recently, she never really thought of him as more than a friend. She always got a laugh out of the things he said during class, and last year they were lab partners in science. But never, in all of that time did she think Matt was, well, *cute*. But then, this summer, she went to the same sleep-away camp as Matt. They sat around the fire at night, sharing ghost stories. During the day, she noticed the way he did flips from the diving board into the pond. Suddenly she started to see him differently. When sitting by the campfire, she felt herself wanting to sit closer to Matt. She wondered what it would be like to hold his hand or feel his arms around her. She started noticing little things about him, like the fact that he had two laughs: one was a quiet laugh that he used when he was being polite, or listening to adults, and the other laugh was big and loud and boomed off the walls. She even wondered what it would be like to kiss him.

Now, she suddenly found herself at a loss for words when she was around him. During meal time at camp, she'd find herself in

ROMANTIC ATTRACTION

When it comes to romance, pretty much everyone, young or old, feels a little nervous.

Romantic attraction is a little like a magnet that pulls us closer to another person. It's hard to resist!

line beside him, and instead of talking easily to him about her day, like she always had before, she stumbled over her words; to cover her nervousness, she laughed too loud. Afterward, she cringed, remembering, and felt like an idiot.

What was going on? Why was it suddenly so difficult to act normal around someone who had been her friend for over a year?

WHAT IS ROMANTIC ATTRACTION?

Sarah is feeling the beginnings of romantic attraction. She's young enough that it's still a new feeling for her, but in a few years, she'll be far more familiar with this emotion.

When a person feels romantic attraction to another person, she wants to be closer to that person, both physically and emotionally.

Heterosexual people will feel romantic attraction to members of the opposite sex, while homosexual people will be attracted to members of the same sex. The feelings are pretty much the same, though!

Romantic attraction is different from the feeling we get when we want someone to be our friend. It's more than that. Sometimes it's a feeling like you want to kiss that person. For others it might simply be a desire to hold hands or look into the other person's eyes. Some people don't want any of that stuff. Each person feels romantic attraction differently. Generally, we break romantic attraction down into different parts so it's easier to talk about. Some people think of romantic attraction as dating, love, and sex.

Dating is a process that can take weeks, months, or even years. You go out to movies, you eat dinner together, or if you're at a younger stage in life, maybe you just spend time walking together through the halls between classes. Dating is a modern term for the way that two people who are attracted to each other get to know one another.

Over time, dating can lead to love. Love is hard to define, of course, and each person will decide for himself when he feels like he's "in love." But love *usually* comes after two people have spent enough time together to know one another and care deeply about that other person.

Finally, sex is a part of romantic attraction. Like love and dating, people have different ideas about when sex is appropriate. It's a big step, and lots of consequences go along with the decision to have sex. You need to be sure you're ready to handle those consequences before you decide to have sex with anyone.

WHO SHOULD BE ATTRACTED TO WHOM?

The examples in this book involve boys and girls who are attracted to each other. But some boys feel attracted to other boys, and some girls are attracted to other girls. Some people feel attracted to both boys and girls, or others don't feel attracted to anyone at all.

Many movies, television, books, and music focus on romantic attraction. In fact, much of the art that's been created by humans is in some way connected to romantic love. It's one of the most powerful emotions we experience as humans. But not everything

Puberty is the physical stage at which your body reaches sexual maturity. Adolescence is the psychological and social phase that begins with puberty and ends with adulthood.

Make Connections

Sexual orientation has to do with the romantic attraction a person feels toward another person. There are several types of sexual orientation.

- Heterosexual: People who are heterosexual are attracted to members of the opposite sex. Heterosexual males are attracted to females, and heterosexual females are attracted to males. Heterosexuals are also called "straight."

- Homosexual: People who are homosexual are attracted to people of the same sex. Females who are attracted to other females are lesbians, while males who are attracted to other males are usually called gay. "Gay" can also refer to both male and female homosexuals.

- Bisexual: People who are bisexual are attracted to members of both sexes.

- Asexual: Adults who don't feel any sexual attraction for anyone are sometimes referred to as asexual. They may not be interested in sex, but they still need to be emotionally close to other people. Adolescents, however, develop sexual attraction feelings at different ages. A person who doesn't feel sexual attraction at fourteen, for example, may experience it when he's a few years older.

you see or read about romance will be true for you. Each person has to chart his or her own course for romantic attraction.

During *adolescence*, a lot of physical changes start happening. Some of these changes are obvious: boys grow beards, their voices get deeper, and their muscles get bigger, while girls grow breasts and other curves. Meanwhile, other changes are going

Research Project

Ask at least ten to twenty adults in your life if they'd be willing to be in a survey. They could be teachers, parents, aunts, uncles, grandparents, or parents of friends. If they're willing, ask them how old they each were the first time they remember feeling romantic attraction. Then make a graph showing the results of your survey. What's the range of ages? Are some ages more common than others?

on inside young adults' brains—and these changes can create all sorts of new emotions. It can be confusing!

Understanding who you're attracted to can be especially confusing sometimes. Young adults may need time to sort out their sexual orientation. Being romantically attracted to someone of the same sex does not necessarily mean you're gay—and being attracted to someone of the opposite sex doesn't always mean you're straight either. It's common—and normal—for teenagers to be attracted to people of the same sex and the opposite sex. Some people might go beyond just feeling attracted and experiment with sexual experiences with people of their own sex or of the opposite sex. These experiences, by themselves, do not necessarily mean that a person is gay or straight. They may be just part of growing up and figuring out who you are. During adolescence, people sort through their feelings, and they figure out various parts of their identities.

WHEN DOES ROMANTIC ATTRACTION BEGIN?

Romantic attraction happens at different ages for different people. Very young children sometimes feel some version of romantic

Text-Dependent Questions

1. Explain the differences between heterosexual, homosexual, bisexual, and asexual.

2. What are the three parts of romantic attraction listed in this chapter?

3. According to this chapter, what changes take place during adolescence?

4. Based on the information provided in this chapter, why do many girls get interested in romantic relationships earlier than boys do?

attraction. However, they're just as likely to be attracted to a make-believe person—like Mighty Mouse or Little Mermaid—as someone real. Not always but often, girls develop feelings of romantic attraction earlier than boys. This can be one reason why girls often date older boys.

There's no "right time" to start feeling romantic attraction. Romantic attraction has a lot to do with your body's *biological* urge to find a sexual mate—and everyone's body develops at different speeds. Again, girls tend to develop sexually a little earlier than boys do. It can be frustrating or confusing if you're watching your friends start dating but you feel left behind. But "normal" comes in lots of different shapes. What's normal for you may not be what's normal for others your age—but that's okay! Normal is whatever is right for you.

HORMONES

Words to Understand

evolution: The process by which living things change over a long time to become more suited to their environments.

researchers: Scientists who try to make new discoveries.

cultural: Having to do with the shared art, ethics, or thoughts of a certain group of people.

genes: The DNA stored in our cells, which contains the code that controls our physical traits. Our genes are passed down from our parents.

TWO

WHAT HAPPENS TO YOU WHEN YOU FEEL ROMANTIC ATTRACTION?

It's the night of the school dance and everything is going well—so far. Matt has managed to avoid making an idiot of himself, dancing in groups with his friends and keeping a big smile on his face. After a while, he realizes the smile is genuine. He really is having a good time. Usually Matt hates these things. School dances can be so boring. But for once the school invited a great DJ, and tonight everyone is laughing and relaxed. Matt keeps his cool, making conversation with both his girl and guy friends. When a certain radio hit comes over the speakers, he even busts out a ridiculous dance move that gets everyone laughing.

But on the inside, Matt's heart is racing. The girl he likes, Sarah, is here tonight, and she looks beautiful. Matt has spent all night avoiding her, trying to stay on the opposite side of the school gymnasium. He's trying to enjoy time with his friends, but all he

ROMANTIC ATTRACTION

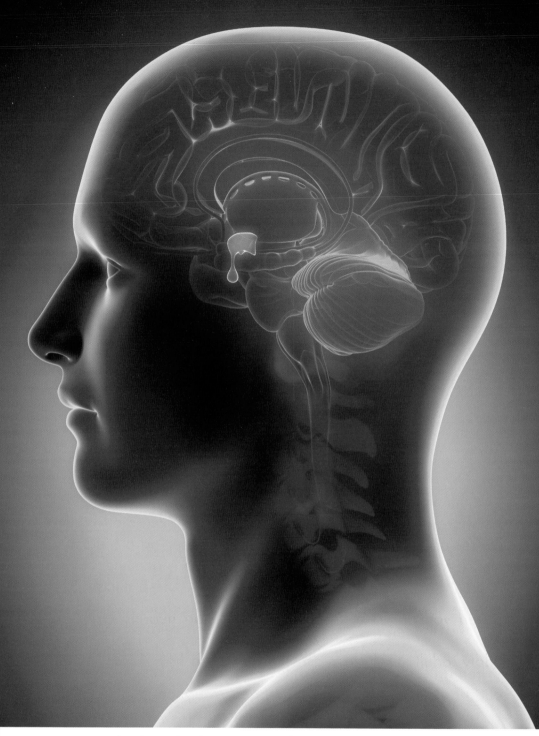

Your pituitary gland is only about the size of a pea—but it's the gland that gets puberty started by sending out hormones that trigger changes throughout your body.

can think about is Sarah. The thought of talking to her makes him feel excited and sick at the same time.

During a break in music, Matt decides to peel off from the group and head to the water fountain. As he exits the dark gym, the bright fluorescent hall lights make him squint. He's letting his eyes adjust to the brightness, when suddenly he realizes he's just about to run straight into Sarah. In fact, he almost knocks her over. She makes a little squeak to warn him, and he pulls up short. He feels himself go white. His heart races, and he can hear his pulse in his ears. He reaches out a hand but then takes it back, realizing his palms are so sweaty that he'd probably gross her out. To his horror, he realizes his entire body is shaking!

THE SCIENCE OF ATTRACTION

What Matt experienced is actually quite normal: the racing heart, the sweaty palms, the shakes. Romantic attraction has a powerful effect on our bodies that comes from thousands of years of *evolution*. From our body's perspectives, it's all leading up to sex.

Think about it: for the human species to continue, we need to make babies. For people to have sex and create children, they need to be attracted to one another. Our bodies are finely tuned to tell us when we see someone who attracts us. Then our brains create a series of chemicals that encourage us to get closer to that person.

THE BRAIN, THE BODY, AND HORMONES

When you get to a certain age, you start hearing a lot about "hormones." In fact, pretty much whenever a teenager acts a little oddly, adults likely to place the blame on hormones. Hormones get blamed for a lot during adolescence!

Actually, hormones are involved in almost every activity we do. Hormones are chemical messengers that travel throughout the body, affecting everything from how you grow to how you react to an attractive person. Hormones are stored in body parts

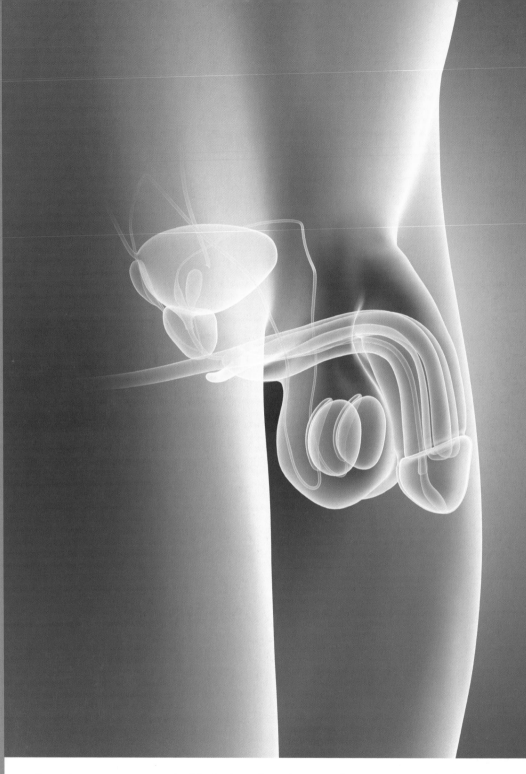

ROMANTIC ATTRACTION

If you're a guy, you probably feel as though most of your romantic feelings start in these organs—but in reality, you have your brain to blame even more.

Make Connections

It may sound gross, but extra testosterone is passed along whenever a man kisses a woman. Testosterone in his saliva may make the woman more attracted to him, unless she really doesn't care for him—and then he may be out of luck!

called glands. These glands make up the endocrine system. The endocrine system sends hormones throughout your body that tell it when to run away from a dangerous animal, when to raise your heart rate, and when it's safe to rest and enjoy a meal.

The brain's cells are full of electrical signals. These signals in the brain are incredibly complex. They process everything that the body senses—sights, smells, sounds, touch. Then it turns the messages from your senses into information we can understand. These messages also trigger other reactions within the brain.

When you see a "cute" boy or girl, a thousand tiny processes occur in your brain in the time that it takes you to blink. All at once, your brain processes everything about that person—body shape, face, voice, smell, hair, everything. Almost instantly, without even thinking about it, you've already decided if you think this person is cute or not.

Let's say you *do* find this person attractive. In the matter of only a few seconds, those electrical signals in your brain start telling your body how to react. This is where hormones enter the picture.

In males, the testes are the glands that make the hormone called testosterone. The female hormone, estrogen, is made in a female's ovaries, but other hormones are made in the ovaries as well. Testosterone and estrogen play a role in romantic attraction. Testosterone is present in both men and women, and studies show that higher levels of testosterone make people more likely to be attracted to a person. Scientists say that testosterone and estrogen

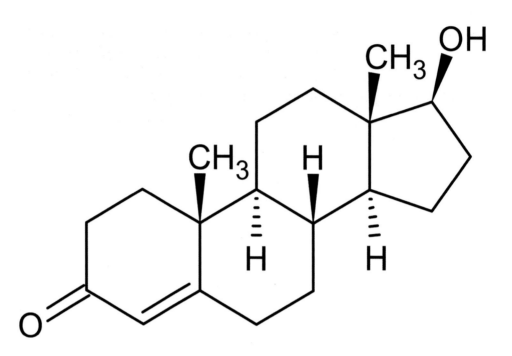

Everything in the world is made up chemicals, which are combinations of atoms and molecules. This diagram shows the chemical structure of testosterone, one of the chemicals responsible for romantic attraction.

are the most important chemicals for the first stage of attraction. Testosterone, especially, is what makes you start looking at other people and trying to make connections. Other "love" chemicals, however, are generated by other glands in the body, and these chemicals are just as important to how attracted (or not attracted!) you feel.

THE ATTRACTION PHASE

Although lots of things are at work in Matt's brain and body, testosterone is one of the biggest factors that brought him to the dance in the first place. Matt knew that Sarah might be at the dance. So let's get back to the moment where Matt and Sarah are almost colliding in the hallway outside the gym.

In that moment, a new "love chemical" comes into play called norepinephrine. This chemical behaves a lot like another chemical called adrenaline. Adrenaline raises our heart rate and prepares us for a fight or a big test. In the same way, norepinephrine shakes us into action too—but instead of getting us ready to fight, it gives us that little extra nudge to talk to that cute girl or boy. Because it acts a lot like adrenaline, though, norepinephrine gives us some of the same side-effects of adrenaline. That explains Matt's sweaty palms and racing heart. In many ways, Matt's body is experiencing something similar to what a person feels when he's hiking a trail and a bear crosses his path. Adrenaline tells the body: "Make a decision right now—fight or run away!" In the same way, every time Matt sees Sarah, norepinephrine surges through his body, saying, "Talk to her! Do *something* to get her attention!" The expression "love at first sight" actually has some science to back it up. When two people meet, and both are attracted to one another, they experience a mutual surge of this chemical that acts like adrenaline. In that moment, they both feel like the person across from them is the only one in the room!

Now let's say Matt and Sarah really hit it off. After the dance, they start spending time together during school, walking to every class together. At this point, other love chemicals start to enter the picture. Dopamine is a chemical that acts a lot like the drug cocaine. It gives us increased energy and less need for food or sleep. It also gives us an increased ability to focus and enjoy the smallest details. Dopamine flows through the bodies of people who are attracted to one another. That explains why people seem to be content to spend so much time together when they first fall in love. In fact, it can be hard to separate them sometimes. Friends

ROMANTIC ATTRACTION

This field vole, one of the few monogamous mammals, may help scientists understand human romance a little better.

Make Connections

In the animal kingdom, not too many mammals are monogamous. To be monogamous means to have only one sexual partner. Prairie voles are mostly monogamous, however, so researchers have studied them to try to make comparisons with humans. When scientists gave prairie voles a drug that decreased vasopressin, they saw a sharp drop in monogamy. Prairie voles began choosing multiple sexual partners.

In another study, scientists gave oxytocin to female rats that had never had sex and had no babies of their own. They wanted to see how oxytocin affected the motherly instinct to bond with offspring. The female rates with high levels of oxytocin spent time fawning over baby rats, nuzzling the little pups and protecting them as if they were their own.

and family complain that they never see Matt and Sarah anymore. They seem to want to only spend time together!

"THE HONEYMOON IS OVER!" AND THE ATTACHMENT PHASE

What motivates us to stay with that person? What happens inside the body of a person who's been in love for weeks or months? Let's follow Matt and Sarah a little further down the road of romantic attraction.

At this point, scientists say that it's all about attachment. Attachment is a longer-lasting commitment. It's what bonds a couple together. There's no exact formula that predicts when a relationship moves from the attraction phase to the attachment phase. It happens differently for everybody. But most experts say it starts to happen after the first four or five months. The rush from norepinephrine and dopamine subsides—which means that being with

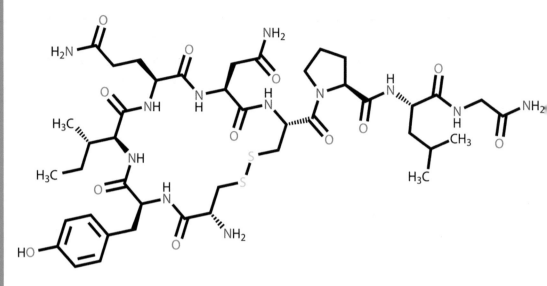

This is a diagram of a molecule of oxytocin—the "love hormone" that helps connect us to each other.

the other person is no longer as exciting. But now other hormones kick into action. Three important hormones regulate this stage of the love game: oxytocin, vasopressin, and serotonin.

Some people call oxytocin the "glue" chemical because it binds people together. Oxytocin isn't limited to people in love. Both mother and child experience a huge rush of oxytocin right after birth. Oxytocin helps bind them together and gives them a peaceful feeling that makes the relationship feel right. In romantic relationships, oxytocin helps bridge the gap after those early emotions start to fade away. After the intensity of the attraction phase, you need a dose of oxytocin to reach the next level. Oxytocin gives you a sense of trust in the other person.

Vasopressin is similar to oxytocin, but vasopressin is less about bonding than it is about satisfaction. Vasopressin makes you feel contented and happy when you're with your romantic partner. Scientists think that vasopressin is important for keeping humans together in the long term. After a few months, Sarah and Matt know a lot about each other. They've spent hundreds of hours together. And yet, if things are going well, they may still feel very attracted to one another. Vasopressin plays a big role in why they continue to feel happy each time they hear the other person's voice.

Serotonin also promotes a warm and fuzzy feeling of being contented with the other person. In fact, when **researchers** studied how serotonin levels changed in people who were in love, they found that serotonin steadily increased over time. After a few months, serotonin levels actually shoot way up. You can look at this as both a good or bad thing. This upshot in serotonin marks the end of that "attraction" phase and the beginning of the "attachment phase." In other words, the honeymoon is over!

EVOLUTION AND ROMANTIC ATTRACTION

Over time humans have developed certain traits that define a beautiful person. Of course, each society has its own *cultural* ideas about what is attractive. What's beautiful in rural China is different from what's beautiful in Sweden or Denmark. But in general, people all over the world find certain physical traits beautiful. In women, this usually has to do with the shape of their hips and breasts. In men, beauty usually means tall and muscular.

That probably doesn't surprise you too much. But here's where it gets interesting. There's a big debate among scientists about *why* we find these traits beautiful. Why aren't we usually attracted to women with wide waists and flat chests or short, skinny men? Many scientists argue that these traits are attractive to us because

Research Project

The text says that dopamine is a brain chemical that acts a lot like cocaine. Using the Internet and the library, research the effects that cocaine has on the brain. Compare and contrast these effects to the effects of dopamine.

they signify health. When we look for a mate, we're unconsciously looking for someone with good *genes* who will give us a healthy baby. Scientists say that humans evolved to become attracted to people who will help them make healthy children. In ancient times, being able to spot a good mate could mean the difference between your family surviving or not. If you picked a weak or unhealthy mate, you might end up with a baby who never survived to adulthood. Spotting a "beautiful" mate was a life-or-death decision!

Other factors besides health may have factored into it. For instance, it turns out that on average, skinnier men live longer than muscular men, who are considered more attractive to women. But in prehistoric times, that muscular man may have been the better bet when it came to protecting and providing for a family. The tall, muscular guy could take down the wooly mammoth and fight off the rival tribes.

Over the millennium, though, other factors have come into play with romantic attraction. A lot of these had to do with how different cultures defined wealth. For example, in ancient China, men found tiny feet attractive in women because it indicated to them that the woman was wealthy and well-born. Some cultures found heavyset women more beautiful than thin women. Today our culture puts a lot of value on thinness as a quality necessary for being attractive.

Text-Dependent Questions

1. How does this chapter connect evolution to romantic attraction?

2. According to this chapter, what roles do the hormones estrogen and testosterone play in romantic attraction?

3. Explain what happens during the attraction phase of a romantic relationship.

4. Explain how the attachment phase is different from the attraction phase.

But despite what our culture says, we each have our definition of what makes someone romantically attractive. One person might like women with big hips, while someone else might define himself as a "breast guy." One person might like men who are a little burly, while someone else might like guys who are tall and thin. Scientists have yet to find an exact definition for what humans find attractive—or why.

Romantic attraction resists definition. Despite all the scientific research that's been done into it, it's still a little mysterious. When it comes right down to it, a poem or song will probably express the feeling far better than any scientist will ever be able to.

Words to Understand

vulnerable: Open to being attacked or hurt.
psychologists: Experts on the mind and emotions.

THREE

How Does Romantic Attraction Affect Your Life?

Romantic attraction can be powerful, so powerful that it affects almost all aspects of your daily life. If you feel strongly for someone, your feelings can affect your appetite, your ability to focus on schoolwork, and much more. All that's pretty normal, especially for young adults. The good news is that romantic attraction changes over time. But as an adolescent, you're probably not ready to settle down with one person for the rest of your life. This means that your relationships may mostly be focused on the early stages of romantic attraction, rather than the later stages. Studies show that for fifteen-year-olds, for example, most romantic relationships last on average only about three to four months.

But that's plenty of time for the attraction to cause you lots of joy, excitement, fear, and pain. When people talk about romantic

The early stages of a romantic relationship, when you're not sure what the other person feels for you, are both scary and exciting.

Falling in love can seem like an explosion in your life, something over which you have no control.

attraction, they often refer to it as "falling in love." This is because, for most people, it doesn't feel like they had much choice about it. They were just minding their own business, living their lives—and then the bottom dropped out! Romantic attraction is something that feels as though we've lost some of our control. It can be both scary and delightful!

When you feel attracted to someone, you're **vulnerable**. You run the risk of getting hurt. Romantic attraction may not break your bones, but it sure can hurt your feelings. It can be painful if the person you like doesn't like you back, or if he decides he's not attracted to you anymore.

Being in love is one of the most exciting experiences in life—and it can be one of the most emotionally rewarding as well.

Thinking about the person you love can add joy to your life even when you're not together.

WHAT ARE THE REWARDS OR ROMANTIC ATTRACTION?

But when romantic attraction goes well, it can be a wonderful experience. Some people even say that romantic love is one of the best things in life. A romantic attraction can make you nervous and uncomfortable at first, but it can lead to feelings of peace and love. When someone returns your feelings, that can make you feel confident and accepted. Romantic attraction can give you energy for life's other tasks. Walking the dog or doing your homework takes on new meaning when you feel like someone out there cares about you and wants to be with you.

The excitement of first love can lead to a new sense of who you are. It's one of the important steps toward adulthood.

Romantic attraction is part of growing up, so it can make you feel older and more mature. Some **_psychologists_** say that romantic love is one of the first steps we take away from our parents. Feeling attracted to someone doesn't mean you don't love your parents anymore, but it does mean that you want to see what it's like to connect with someone outside your family. It's a normal step in the growing-up process.

WHAT ARE THE RISKS?

You may feel that you're ready for romantic attraction before your parents think you are. One of the biggest reasons that parents

Text-Dependent Questions

1. Explain three "rewards" of romantic attraction listed in this chapter.

2. What does the text say are the two categories of danger involved with romantic attraction? Explain each one.

3. According to this chapter, what did evolution design romantic attraction to lead to?

4. How does the text indicate that sex plays a different role in the modern world compared to what it did thousands of years ago?

make such a big fuss over dating is because they know that dating can hurt their children. Even when two people have the same feelings for one another, things can get tricky. The dangers of romantic attraction fall into two categories: emotional and physical.

Romantic attraction can sometimes lead to sex. That's what it's designed to do from an evolutionary point of view. But sex isn't as simple today as it was thousands of years ago when humans were evolving. Back then, sex was just about making as many babies as possible, so that the human species would survive in the midst of a dangerous and challenging world. Today, though, our world works differently. Young people need education and other life experiences before they're ready to settle down and raise families. You'll probably start experiencing romantic attraction long before you're ready to have a baby! But sex without the proper protection leads to pregnancy. In today's world, it can also lead to sexually transmitted diseases (STDs). These are serious physical consequences that can result from romantic attraction.

Having a boyfriend break up with you and hurt you is one of love's risks. It's times like those when you especially need your friends!

Research Project

Using the Internet and the library, research what romantic attraction looked like in an earlier era. Focus on one era in one geographical region, such as the nineteenth century in the United States or the Middle Ages in Europe. What words were used to described romantic attraction then? (For example, "dating" is a term that was never used until the twentieth century.) What behaviors were acceptable back then for young people who were attracted to each other romantically—and what weren't? At what age were young people expected to marry? Compare and contrast romantic attraction today with the era you researched. How is still the same? How is it different today?

There are emotional consequences as well. Romantic attraction can leave you feeling stressed. It can interfere with your ability to concentrate on school work. You may miss out on other life opportunities because you're so preoccupied with your romantic feelings. Romantic attraction can lead to people making themselves vulnerable to each other, in ways that they wouldn't otherwise. Think about it at the crudest level: there's no way you would take your clothes off for someone normally, but romantic attraction can make you do all sorts of things! Being vulnerable with someone you love can be a wonderful experience that leads to closeness and bonding—but what if the other person isn't mature enough for that kind of bonding? If you're ready and she isn't, you can end up feeling pretty devastated emotionally. And the more vulnerable you've made yourself—the more you've exposed yourself both physically and emotionally—the more it's likely to hurt if the relationship doesn't work out.

Words to Understand

exclusive: Limited to one person; not shared with anyone else.

intense: Having very strong feelings or opinions; extremely serious.

abusive: Involving frequent violence and cruelty.

FOUR

LEARNING FROM ROMANTIC ATTRACTION

Dating can be scary. You worry the other person won't like you. You worry you'll do something stupid. You worry you're not pretty or good looking enough.

All those worries are normal. When it comes to romantic attraction, it may all seem new and strange to you—but people have been feeling the same things for thousands of years. Pretty much everyone survives these confusing, terrifying, and exciting feelings!

Many studies show that teens take dating too seriously. When romantic attraction strikes, it can seem like the only important thing in the world. After all, it is a very powerful emotion. Everything else may fade in comparison.

Think about two of the most famous teenage lovers in the world: Romeo and Juliet. They met each other and instantly fell madly in love—and then became so obsessed with their feelings, that their

Romeo and Juliet's intense love-at-first-glance made more sense in the 1600s than it does today in the twenty-first century.

story ended with them both dead. Their story may be fictional, but real-life teenagers often feel that same sense of life-and-death desperation when they're in love.

Psychologists suggest that adolescents need to step back and take a longer view at their lives. Remember that dating is not about finding the person with whom you will spend the rest of your life. The person you love so madly today may not matter much at all to you in just a few months' time. Breaking up or ending a relationship doesn't need to be a big deal. It might seem like the end of the world, but it's not. In fact, very few people marry someone they dated in middle or high school.

Psychologists also recommend that young adults get to know lots of people rather than commit themselves to *exclusive* relationships too young. In Romeo and Juliet's world, where people got married when they were in their early teens, that kind of *intense* relationship made more sense—but in the twenty-first century, most people aren't ready to commit to one person permanently until they are in their twenties or even their thirties. Going to college and establishing a career is hard work, and you may not have the energy for it if you're already spending most of your time with one person. Young adults who form committed, exclusive relationships may also miss out on other friendships and experiences. Experts recommend that teenagers interact in groups rather than spending lots of time alone in couples. Romantic attraction is powerful stuff so it's good to keep those emotions balanced in settings where you can set up boundaries to protect yourself and have fun at the same time.

Finally, make sure you set those boundaries ahead of time. Decide what kind of sexual activity, if any, is appropriate for you, and don't let anyone change your mind. Have a plan for how to end the date if you get uncomfortable. Don't wait until you're in the situation to decide what to do. Romantic attraction triggers strong emotional reactions in your brain, as we discussed in chapter 2, and those reactions get in the way of more rational thought. So do your thinking ahead of time!

What if you give your heart away—and the other person doesn't want it? It's a good idea to be careful when you first fall in love.

UNREQUITED LOVE

Unrequited love—feeling attracted to someone who doesn't feel the same way—can be a painful experience. It can be just as uncomfortable for the person who doesn't return the feelings. When two friends are in this situation, it can be even more difficult.

Take Franklin and Katie, for example. They met about three weeks ago on the first day of school when the teacher assigned them to sit next to each other in math class. Katie had a crush on Franklin the moment she saw him. Franklin doesn't really find Katie all that cute, but he does need someone to help him study math, and Katie is one of the best students in class. Over the next three weeks the two spend hours together working on math problems. Franklin is learning a lot from Katie, but he's starting to suspect that Katie has romantic feelings for him. Lately she's been getting a little too close when she leans over his shoulder to show him an equation.

Finally, Katie tells him the truth, and Franklin is horrified. Even worse, he finds himself telling Katie an outright lie: he tells her he thinks she's really cute, but that right now he doesn't want to be more than friends. This totally confuses Katie. She believes he's attracted to her, so she hopes she can change his mind. Over the next few weeks, she continues to look for chances to be alone with Franklin. He wants to keep studying math with her, but she wants more than that. Katie begins to wonder what she should do differently.

In the end, things become so awkward between them that Franklin starts avoiding Katie. During math class, he won't even look in her direction. After a few weeks, they stop talking altogether. Katie feels crushed. But it could have gone a little differently. Katie and Franklin could have built a strong relationship that wasn't built on romantic attraction—but neither of them went that route.

Alice and Pete, however, are good friends who feel comfortable around each other. Alice tells Pete a lot of secrets about her life, including boys she likes. Pete trusts Alice with personal stuff

It can be easy to misinterpret a relationship. What one person considers to be only a friendship can seem like something more to the other person. Being both honest and respectful of the other person's feelings is the best way to save the friendship.

Make Connections

51

One out of eleven high school students report being physically hurt by a date.

Learning from Romantic Attraction

from his life, too. He tells her about other girls he likes, and he tells her his hopes and dreams for the future. They know a lot about each other, and yet they've never gone on a single date or kissed even once. They both play in the school jazz band and they both hate sports. Basically, they have a lot in common, and they enjoy each other's friendship. They like each other for lots of reasons, and they trust each other.

Then one day things start to change between them. Alice starts noticing that Pete seems more and more attractive to her. She's always thought he was cute, but now she gets really distracted by the romantic attraction she's feeling for him. She likes the way he makes her feel, and she wants to be more than just friends. At first she ignores her new feelings. She doesn't want to ruin the good friendship that's made her so happy. And what if Pete doesn't feel the same way? But she can't ignore her feelings any longer. She's starting to act strange around Pete. She's even been acting mean to him lately! Finally she works up the courage to tell Pete how she really feels.

On the big day, Pete is packing up his saxophone case after jazz band practice. Alice waits nervously for him in the hall, tapping her foot. When Pete finally walks around the corner, she practically attacks him with, "I think we need to talk!" Pete agrees to join her outside, in a little alley between two buildings. There, Alice tells Pete all that's been running through her mind. Pete looks a little surprised, but he's not upset. He thanks Alice for being honest with him and says that he had noticed her acting different lately. Then he gives the bad news: he doesn't feel the same way.

Studies show that many teenage girls feel pressured to have sex or engage in sexual acts with their boyfriends. Nearly 25 percent of all teenage girls say that they have gone further sexually in a relationship than they wanted to.

He's complimented, though, and he wants to remain friends—but he makes it clear that he doesn't have any of the same feelings for Alice.

Alice goes home feeling sick with disappointment, feeling foolish that she ever thought Pete might feel the same way. But over the next few days she begins to feel better, lighter somehow. Letting Pete know how she feels is like getting a burden off her back. Now she waits to see if Pete will act any differently toward her. On Friday, as she's packing up her trumpet, she bumps into him. He's been waiting for her outside the band room. "Hey!" he says. "Let's talk."

Pete and Alice continue to enjoy their friendship. Pete lets Alice know he truly values her friendship, even though he's not attracted to her romantically. Months later, things are back to normal between them. Alice can even laugh when she remembers how attracted to him she was for a while.

What made the difference between their experience and Katie and Franklin's? A couple of things. For one thing, Pete was honest about his feelings. He didn't lead Alice on or give her false hope. But maybe most important, their friendship had a strong foundation. They liked and respected each other. They cared about each other. Franklin, on the other hand, wanted to use Katie's math knowledge, but he didn't really care about her as a person. And Katie took a leap and made herself vulnerable to him before she really knew if she could trust him.

Important warning signals of an abusive relationship include:

- if someone harms you physically in any way.
- if someone threatens to harm you, even if he or she doesn't carry out the threats.
- if someone tries to control different aspects of your life, such as how you dress, who you're friends with, where you go, and what you say.
- if someone puts you down or makes you feel bad about yourself.
- if someone threatens to hurt himself/herself if you break up.
- if someone gets angry and jealous over innocent actions, such as when you talk to someone in the hall or work on a school project with someone.
- if someone tries to manipulate you (for example, by saying, "If you loved me, you would. . .")

WHEN ROMANTIC ATTRACTION GOES WRONG

Healthy relationships are always built on respect and trust. But that kind of relationship takes maturity—and not every young adult has the level of maturity needed. As a result, some relationships can go wrong and become *abusive*.

Abuse can be physical or emotional. Any time someone does something to you that involves violence—whether it's hitting or shoving or pulling your hair—it's probably a form of physical abuse. Emotional abuse can be harder to recognize sometimes. It includes things like teasing and insults, but it could also be threats or humiliating someone. People in relationships are bound to hurt

It is never okay for someone to hurt you physically. People who truly love you would never use violence against you.

each other sometimes—none of us are perfect—but abuse is when a person makes a habit of treating you in a way that makes you feel bad.

Sometimes young adults mistake abusive behavior for love. Jennifer, for example, felt complimented when her girlfriend Becky was jealous of her. At first, Jennifer liked it when Becky would get angry if she talked to someone else. She felt it proved how much Becky loved her. But after a while, Jennifer started to feel smothered. She realized that Becky treated her as though she were a possession, rather than a person in her own right. Becky didn't respect her enough to let her make her own decisions about who she wanted be friends with. Also, Becky scared her a little when she was angry. When Becky was feeling jealous, she would sometimes grab Jennifer so hard she left bruises on Jennifer's arms.

Make Connections

A nasty relationship can be one of the worst experiences for a human being. It can make us lose our trust in not just the person who hurt us but also other people who might otherwise be our friends. Be kind to your friend who is going through a tough breakup or is recovering from a bad relationship. Listen without judging her, and don't cast doubt on what she tells you. Give her the benefit of the doubt and remind her that she doesn't deserve to be abused. Encourage your friend to reach out to an adult and get help. Be there for her when she feels alone or unsafe. Be patient and understand it may take weeks or months for her to recover. Finally, never confront her abuser! Starting a fight can be dangerous and totally unhelpful. It's much better if you enlist the help of an adult or an authority.

Healthy romantic relationships are always built on respect—and real love involves trust, on both sides. Jennifer knew she had the right to be treated with respect. She knew she also had the right not be physically or emotionally harmed by another person. She talked to her friends and a counselor at school, and eventually, she decided to break up with Becky.

Lisa had another problem in her relationship with Aaron: he constantly pressured her to have sex with him. Lisa liked kissing Aaron and snuggling with him. She liked the way he made her body feel. But she wasn't ready to have sex. But Aaron insisted if she really loved him, she would "go all the way." Lisa felt guilty for not having sex with him—but she also felt uncomfortable thinking about having sex. She felt confused and scared—but Aaron wouldn't listen to her when she tried to tell him how she felt. Sometimes she felt angry with him, but other times she felt flattered that he wanted her so much. She felt as though it proved he really loved her. But by pressuring Lisa, Aaron was showing he didn't

Respect is an essential element in all romantic relationships. If anything about the relationship makes you uncomfortable, take a look at your boundaries. Maybe you need to define them more clearly, both for yourself and for the other person.

really respect her. He was trying to use Lisa to satisfy his own sexual feelings, rather than caring about what was best for her.

Adolescents experience emotions very strongly. It's how their brains are made, and it's normal. But it also means you need to protect yourself from people who could make you feel intense hurt and unhappiness. Set up boundary lines in your relationships: know what's acceptable to you in a relationship and what isn't— and then stick to your decision. Don't make yourself too emotionally vulnerable.

Setting up boundary lines likes these in relationships is an important way to protect yourself, both physically and emotionally. Teens who don't have healthy boundaries that protect themselves from getting hurt can get in trouble, both emotionally and physically. A bad relationship can make you feel sad and confused. It can get in the way of other relationships, and it can even hurt your grades. Sometimes, it can lead to drug and alcohol abuse

- Think over what you want and why you want it. Take time to think through your feelings and the reasons for your decision.

- Do what's best for you; be true to yourself. Even if the other person might be hurt by your decision, it's okay to do what's right for you.

- Think about the other person's feelings. You probably can't avoid hurting him or her—but be as kind and respectful as you can. Let the other person know he or she still matters to you.

- Be honest—but that doesn't mean cruel. Don't insult the other person. Let him or her know the good things you'll remember about your relationship. Say the things you still like about the person, even though you're no longer romantically attracted.

- Be clear. Don't try to be so kind that you give the person mixed messages. Make sure he or she knows that your mind is made up about ending the relationship.

- Break up in person. Don't use e-mail or Facebook. Don't text your breakup.

or other risky behaviors. Some teenagers who are in bad relationships may hurt themselves, by eating too much or too little, by cutting themselves, or even by considering suicide. So if something in a romantic relationship doesn't feel right, stick up for yourself. Speak up—and if the other person won't listen, get out of the relationship.

Research Project

Make a poster that shows a list of rights and responsibilities for romantic attraction. For example: "I have the right to make up my own mind about when to have sex," and "I have the responsibility to treat my girlfriend or boyfriend with respect." Use this chapter to get you started, but also use the Internet and library to get more ideas. Ask friends, teachers, and family members for their ideas as well. If possible, talk to agencies that provide counseling or shelter for people who are in abusive relationships. List at least ten rights and ten responsibilities. Be as specific as you can.

GETTING OUT OF A SCARY RELATIONSHIP

If you find yourself in a bad relationship, a first step is usually to reach out to a friend, a family member, or teacher. Talk to someone you trust. Tell *someone* what's going on and why you're worried. If you're feeling ashamed that you got yourself into a bad situation, find someone who will remind you that you are not to blame. An abusive partner can make you feel like it's your fault but *it's not your fault*. No one, no matter what, deserves abuse.

Once you make the decision to get out of the relationship, take some practical steps to stay safe. For starters, break up in a public place with friends nearby to support you. Surround yourself with trusted loved ones. Consider changing your school route or locker location. Talk to your parents or someone at school and ask for advice on staying safe inside and outside of school. Use a buddy system when you go places, especially in those first weeks after the breakup. Choose safe places to hang out. Focus on staying positive.

Text-Dependent Questions

1. According to this chapter, why shouldn't young adults commit themselves to exclusive relationships?

2. Describe three examples of a physically abusive relationship given in this chapter.

3. Explain three examples given in this chapter of someone not showing respect to the other person in a romantic relationship.

4. List four warning signals of an abusive relationship, according to the sidebar in this chapter.

5. What are five ways this chapter indicates a bad romantic relationship might hurt someone?

WHAT ROMANTIC RELATIONSHIPS CAN TEACH YOU

Romantic relationships are opportunities to get to know others—and at the same time, you'll learn things about yourself. Even relationships that end badly or that hurt you in some way can teach you important things. You'll learn what you want in a relationship. You learn what you like and what you don't like. You'll understand others better. Loving relationships based on respect teach us to value ourselves more. They build our self-esteem and confidence. They help us grow up and get ready for lifelong commitments.

Find Out More

IN BOOKS

Andrews, Linda Wasmer. *Emotional Intelligence*. New York: Scholastic, 2004.

Eastham, Chad. *The Truth About Dating, Love, and Just Being Friends*. New York: Thomas Nelson, 2011.

Miles, Al. *Ending Violence in Teen Dating Relationships*. Minneapolis, Minn.: Fortress Press, 2005.

Morrison, Betsy S. *Self-Esteem*. New York: Rosen Publishing, 2011.

Spilsbury, Richard. *Emotions: From Birth to Old Age*. Portsmouth, N.H.: Heinemann, 2013.

ONLINE

KidsHealth: Talking About Your Feelings
kidshealth.org/kid/feeling/thought/talk_feelings.html

KidsHealth: Understanding Your Emotions
kidshealth.org/teen/your_mind/emotions/understand-emotions.html

Palto Alto Medical Foundation: Emotions and Life
www.pamf.org/teen/life

PBS: This Emotional Life
www.pbs.org/thisemotionallife

Healthy Teen Network
www.healthyteennetwork.org

Series Glossary of Key Terms

adrenaline: An important body chemical that helps prepare your body for danger. Too much adrenaline can also cause stress and anxiety.

amygdala: An almond-shaped area within the brain where the flight-or-flight response takes place.

autonomic nervous system: The part of your nervous system that works without your conscious control, regulating body functions such as heartbeat, breathing, and digestion.

cognitive: Having to do with thinking and conscious mental activities.

cortex: The area of your brain where rational thinking takes place.

dopamine: A brain chemical that gives pleasure as a reward for certain activities.

endorphins: Brain chemicals that create feelings of happiness.

fight-or-flight response: Your brain's reaction to danger, which sends out messages to the rest of the body, getting it ready to either run away or fight.

hippocampus: Part of the brain's limbic system that plays an important role in memory.

hypothalamus: The brain structure that gets messages out to your body's autonomic nervous system, preparing it to face danger.

limbic system: The part of the brain where emotions are processed.

neurons: Nerve cells found in the brain, spinal cord, and throughout the body.

neurotransmitters: Chemicals that carry messages across the tiny gaps between nerve cells.

serotonin: A neurotransmitter that plays a role in happiness and depression.

stress: This feeling that life is just too much to handle can be triggered by anything that poses a threat to our well-being, including emotions, external events, and physical illnesses.

Index

About the Author & Consultant

Z.B. Hill is an author and publicist living in Binghamton, New York. He has a special interest in adolescent education.

Cindy Croft is director of the Center for Inclusive Child Care at Concordia University, St. Paul, Minnesota where she also serves as faculty in the College of Education. She is field faculty at the University of Minnesota Center for Early Education and Development program and teaches for the Minnesota on-line Eager To Learn program. She has her M.A. in education with early childhood emphasis. She has authored *The Six Keys: Strategies for Promoting Children's Mental Health in Early Childhood Programs* and co-authored *Children and Challenging Behavior: Making Inclusion Work* with Deborah Hewitt. She has worked in the early childhood field for the past twenty years.

Picture Credits